Into the Shadow
of
Doubt

A Collection of Poems

by Shel Craig

For
Lisa & Dave
Tina
Faron
Dave & Deanna
and most especially, Chris

And
for any who believe in the power of words

INTRODUCTION

My poetry often comes from a dark place, and for the most part, this collection is no exception. It's a strange thing to find inspiration from what are perceived to be negative emotions, but all emotion is a worthy source of inspiration and exploration.

In this book, I have included poems that examine fear, judgment, creativity, contemplation and introspection. I hope that you enjoy them, and that they inspire you to explore your own emotions with a sense of curiosity and willingness for discovery.

Best wishes,

Shel

INTROSPECTION

Untitled

I wish I could stir my breath
Or stop it
As easily as poisoned thoughts
Eke out their living

As easily as their snarls
Reach my inner ears,
Whispers I can't hear
But comprehend

Dragged along
The ends of words
Though still unheard,
Tickling every organ

Fed solely on the disconnect,
The discontent of troubled minds
Spit in ears
And stored for future projects

Into the Shadow of Doubt

I rolled my desires into one long scroll,
enough to pave the way to a mountain
I once climbed with my dad
before I knew who I was.
Before I longed for the life I was told couldn't be

Reasoned reminders.
set out on the table, at odd times,
a church-bell call to the summit.
Give not to yourself—
o selfish one,
that gazes on a dream with envy.
It is not yours to declare

For you are placed at the heap
and lowly tread, with the washing.
Be still and be bothered.
It was all too real

'Til I filled myself up,
each morsel savored,
as though it were seasoned
by gods.

I took it, and looked up into
milky blue eyes,
sad and weary, and
utterly spent.

I don't know why she bothered.
A task? A job?
Work hard and endure…
all the wrath god bestows on the poor?

It seemed a philosophy
a condition
a sentence.

But I worshipped at their toes,
mingled in the sleep of their conversation,
and tried to catch the fire that burned
between them… and fizzled.

I choked out one last
smoky remorse
then settled into the ash.

My Castle

It still hangs like drapery
Heavy cloth,
moth-eaten and dusty.
Its edges lay in pools on the floor
Dusty creases
piled on dulled marble.
My castle...
Weather-beaten outside
and in.
The milky shadows...
noon sun through old glass
Thickened, bubbled.
Out of proportion.
Distorted scenes,
of fiery banners and pitchforks,
cling to cold stone.
Like they would have 600 years ago.
Abutted by pastoral pictures.
Quieter times, pleasant times,
when war or its threat lay dormant.
When the drapes were new.
And the panes as clear as
skyscrapers

New Limbs

I dreamt I could see
my breath in midsummer.
Smoke-filled crystals
melting midair.

And woke, for a while,
at the foot of a mountain,
near a crystalline lake
under perilous sky.

Clouds carved the treetops,
sun singed the hills.
But near the cool water,
my breath nearly stilled.

In the footsteps of strangers,
on shadowy banks,
where glacial deposits
transformed icy sills.

Down in the well,
Down in the well
Surface recovered,
from deep in the well

I carved my new limbs
and walked for a mile,
deep in the forest,
where my old body'd died.

Purified sunshine,
warmed with the rain,
and rested,
to wear out again.

Doppelgänger

My doppelgänger's come to call.
Me to myself.
Home to rest.
Art hung high,
in deference.
Strawberry hair
and ruby dress.

In darker times,
she calls—

When all seems lost,
when time has stilled,
when rooms become
hermetically sealed,
doors are barred,
the silence, ill…

She comes to call.

She calls me in.

Untitled

Breath whispered across the miles.
Ruthless, stingy, condescending.
Stings as though it were my own
curated for my collection.

Like a woollen sweater in July,
it tints me.
Spares my spoken self its meaning.
Who else would weather on...
in contradiction?

But strike up the band.
Play me onto the field,
so all can see my misery
in full spectacle.

I wouldn't have it any other way,
it seems.
And yet...

For one taste of magic,
sweet, effervescent joy,
I'd pledge my life.

Ticker tape

I wish I could
take the sting of anger
from my voice

Languishing jealousy
delivered as wisdom
but hidden from me

under dark masses
tended without thought.
Flourishing

I am weak or weakened
by envy, masked
as knowledge

its true evil, obvious,
once the words have tumbled
like ticker tape.

Temptress

I could slip so easily…
back into her arms.
One sly suggestion
one nefarious thought
one glance, too long,
in the mirror

One snide comment
 in a crowded hall
or one damning look
 mailed across the room…
and I could greet her, like a friend

It's tempting…
to pull the curtains,
bolt the door,
and recede to my dungeon
deep in the depths,
where light is just
a memory.

Slimy walls,
moss-filled cracks,
moisture running
to pools where
the silverfish lap.

But I've worked so hard…
scrubbing, scouring,
and coaxing the light
to my rooms

And yet…
I could still be tempted to
kiss her,
and be coddled,
To bury my mind in ease…
with the lies she breathes
like a self-professed prophet.

CREATIVITY

Burned Upon Death

Would they know me
If there was nothing left?
If everything I'd ever done
Was burned upon my death?

Light a match
For every word,
For every note
I ever hit,

I wonder...

Who are we
If there is nothing left?
If everything we'd ever done
was burned upon our deaths?

Strike a match
For every deed
For every promise
Ever kept.

Spark

Barely breathing
On a whim
Lights out and waiting
on enlightenment

The gentle hand
that drapes to earth
and pulls us
from our troubles

Is it real or…
have I done it wrong?
The night still burns
like cold fire

And feels no gentler,
No closer to the spark
that lights imagination
at its will

I'm at its mercy.
Grateful and unyielding
to the bribes
of token gestures

Preventive Poetry

Every time I thought of leaving
a poem came to mind...
quenching the desire to run

Out of town,
to the store,
to anywhere the weight of
work...

Would leave me
in the destitute arms of
boredom

Dickinson's Garden

My thoughts are tumbled,
Uneven and restless
Aching for release...
Into the wild

They wrap me
Night and day, Day and night...
Rearranged
Into reasonable sentiment

Are my words...
Too serpentine? Too shiny?
Too rich to be swallowed
In little bites?

I don't know.

But the ease of unknowing
deepens...
'Til I'm sitting in Dickinson's garden
Contemplating solitude

Beaks Held Wide

The agony
of letting love fall in your lap
with the pain of errant song
from nether corners

darkening the halls
or lighting roman candles
their noisy chant
will push you where you let it

Follow, follow, out the door
into sacred, foreign temples
or dangle from a mountain ledge
one…two fingers keeping grip

while the vultures circle
beaks held wide
close, aloft,
and patient

'til you tumble, tumble
among the willows
to bullrush crowned
by stagnant water

and off again to other lands,
other sights,
other sounds
wherever they may lead you…

While the vultures circle
beaks held wide,
close, aloft
and patient.

Giant X

Some days
I want to burn it all down
carve a giant x
through all that I've done
then watch, amused
as life walks on…

Because inside,
there's a village of lies
etched in the folds
deep in my mind
don't want to believe,
but some days they're right…

When nothing matters
and nothing gives
it's hard to hold on
so close to the edge
down the same dusty road
I was taught never ends…

FEAR

Afraid

I'm afraid.
Damp and chilly
Deep-in-my-bones afraid
Bled and scorched,
Icy sting and
Wind-burned afraid
Melted, withered
Absent sight,
Hold my breath
Until daylight
Curled
And crossed,
In vacant night
Claustrophobic.
Afraid.

But I still breathe.
I still stand.
And I still ache
To fill my shoes.

Open Time

Into the cloud
And out
Posted in wit,
An honest remark
Restlessly forgetful
Of its journey

Strong light and
 Imagery
Brought it to rest
In your thoughts...
Now discomforted

Too much to share,
To shed
To reveal at your doorstep
When you lay
Beside me
In open time

Time Limit

There are only so many days,
Hours, years.
I can no longer spend them
As though
unlimited.

They don't belong to parents,
Friends, or society,
They belong to me.
And they don't ease anxiety
When used to comfort theirs.

I've spent them all to this point.
Some well. Some wasted.
Granted access
To those who claim to know me best,
But know me least.

I've wasted weeks
Debating my intentions.
Though I'd found my home,
No one saw the light
That touched my temples.

I kept it safe.
I kept it close
So I wouldn't have
To let it go.

But time runs out…
And I cannot face it boldly
in their measure

Chameleon

I'm a chameleon
In a crowd
Buttered up,
And dressed to fill a role.
Poured like scotch
Into willing glasses

I fall this way in company.
The arrogance,
Unleashed desire
To be part of something
To become…
Something I am not

Words collide with being
Phrases clothed,
Countenance weakened
Dark but colorful,
Dressed for the occasion

Wearing Thought (Internal Conversation)

Do I go out in the mist
Or stay safely huddled?
Free of the potential
of society
from exposure
or judgment...

Or am I cowering?
Clenched to the dream
of redemption...
hidden from flaws.

So I joined the living,
Briefly,
Wrapped in the fog,
the dampened spring

Life teetered and twittered
along,
swung and shuffled
on pounded asphalt.

And I saw a woman.
Judgment etched her face
Replete with craggy crevices of
decades-old self-condemnation

Lemon-lime
vinegar thoughts
unreasoned and literate
carelessly heaped
for full effect

JUDGMENT

Without Need of Intervention

Why am I so easy to break?
One glowering glance…
One ugly word
and I'm pitched…
…dismantled…
as though there were truth
in the implication.

But I'm whole.
Without need of intervention…
Without need of commentary…
And they're lost
in self-condemnation…
and the abhorrent satisfaction
of causing injury.

I'm whole without them…
I am whole without them.

And they are vested
 in the keeping of scores…
the balancing of pain
projected, and placed
feet forward,
against defeat
with utter senselessness.

Portrait of Judgment

Sometimes fuel,
it seems
Piercing eyes and jowl cheeks
Mounded lips,
Dry river beds
That flow from nose
To crest of lip
Chin juts out and
Fills the mask
Parched but somehow
Seeping bile
Tight and cracked,
Revolting treads
That run 'til they've
reached
End of life.

Monday

The cloak's become a veil
Gauzy and whimpering
A lonely dog at the window.
Morning invites it, like mist,
To settle, keep me still
She's harsh, uncouth
Nasty as the worst school bully.

Like those women on the train,
Offended by the reader in search of a quiet spot
They called after her like third graders—
What's the matter, baby? Did we hurt your feelings?
I'm paraphrasing...

The light that glinted in the large one's eyes
Could slice red meat.
Salivating blood
At the reader's retreat…

It's true...they never leave.
They migrate.
To taller buildings and better clothes...
And walled-in fields,
Where the quarry lay
  within reach.

Politics keeps mouths sewn shut.
Each day, dollars more to come,

Quiet prey 'til they've had enough
A gasp for air or one last punch…

Then they'll stalk the halls for fresher game

Last Cold Night

I watched as winter
Passed me by
Wind-whipped flakes
And frigid nights
Wrapped up
In the clothes I owned
Blankets,
Found along the road

Temperate days
That hardly breathed
Or slept among the
Shy debris
I cast my glances
At the meek
And measured men
Who pass my keep

Goodbye, my love
It's been a treat
Though your cruelty
Brings its own relief
For I fear the night
Shall wrest my bed
And steal the light
That feeds my flesh

'Til my body stills

And the ego soars
To heaven, I hope,
Or somewhere warm
To temperate times
On other planes
Where I can look
Upon the calm

And send love
To my hardened friends
Treads worn softly
Past makeshift beds,
Where summer pleads
Their darting gaze,
They'll find their hearts
With the bitter winds

Restoration

There's a table full of candles
In the room that we just left
Melted teardrops, blackened wicks
Gone cold

Windows armed in satin
Threshold left unswept
Dust kicked in the corner
By the chair

Moonlight skips through moth holes
Kisses mottled mirror
Too far gone to dance
Around the room

A single dusty sliver
Cast on sooty brick
Where furry bodies might have lazed
Or slept

All left without witness
Settled in with time
Patiently awaiting
Restoration

Circus

Death march of circus animals
night strung 'cross their cages
pinned and gagged
in parking lots
awaiting bitter light

Poked and prodded
unpaid servants
balanced over barrels
marched upon and dragged along
by men in ruthless garb

Staring out the night
breathing carbon vapors
on straw-man fondled flooring
willing out the quake

CONTEMPLATION

Tiger Lilies

There's a path to Mt Benson
At the top of Ninth Street
Hidden between forest and suburbia
Or there used to be...

A long pebbled walk
Up, up, up the mountain's side
Past grassy fields dotted with tiger lilies

I wanted to pick them,
Take them home
Or dig them up
So I could keep the memory close

But my dad taught me
That nature is best left where it lies
One piece only a part of the whole.

On we climbed,
My dad nudging me upward,
In increments
'Til we were above ocean,
Above the city,
Just below clouds

My dad sighed
And I knew he could stay there forever
Sleeping under the starlight
And dining on the blue-green mist from below

But we slowly made our way...
Home
Past the grassy fields, where I counted tiger lilies.
And wondered how they got there
But curiously, never asked…

A Day at the Beach

Easy going or dive right in?

Head under and soaked...
I'd stand on one foot
Toes tapping sand
In a slow-motion dance
Teeth chattering & arms wrapped
Like a blanket

Mom stood on the shore
Because the ocean could take you
If you weren't careful...
Or so I'd been told.
    I wasn't scared

I wiggled my toes in
The icy undercurrent
With parfait levels,
Cool to warm
Swirling around me

And I thought about life
That swam or skittered
Ocean or shore…
Jade bodies with hematite eyes
That worshipped and
Warded us off

I Want to Tell You...

how the smell of fresh-cut grass,
slightly damp,
musty,
filled my nose
as I walked down the stairs

...how the shade
betrayed the sun
in the cloudless sky,
the breeze cool for July
The grasses are waving,
the lawn a little too tall
but too short to mow

I'm allergic...
and I sneezed...
my cheekbones ached
but I love the smell
It smells of summer
Not quite like saltwater...
but as close as I'll get here.

Paris, Found

Wide streets and sleek alleys...
In the heart of a mountain
Or industrial-lined roadways
Dandelion-pocked concrete near rusted frost fencing
And newly painted shutters
Black and shiny as their bridges
I'm transplanted in parks with
Tall pigeon-covered statues of mighty men
Hydro towers like Eiffel strung along highways
With Champ de Mars fields below
Not manicured
The trees are organic except in the suburbs
Taller and fanciful in their own way
Here, the sidewalks are perfectly pressed
New and still studying
And I sometimes wonder if it was all a dream
It seems long ago
That the grey-green infusion
Made light of the beauty of industry
The people its color
The sun often elusive
And yet, my heart rested

Rural Route

On a lonely lane,
Worn and pitted
Dried out and dusty
Like vague memory

Of mud-spattered T-shirts
Hung in a yard
Line-dried and brilliant,
Sun-bleached and baked

Shin-level grasses,
And untended beds,
An overturned wagon
With one wheel astray

Wailing footsteps
Lead up to a door
That crackles whenever
The latch leaves the frame

Fertilizer

Ah spring,
the gentle spin
of cleansing rain
over weeks, months...
churning the aromatic memory
of winter's deposits
Four-legged missionaries
sent to fertilize earth
by two-footed giants
too rushed...
to retrieve their gift

Naked

I've felt this before.
Last June.
When earth bared its flaws to the sun,
In prayer.

The beautiful bared themselves
To scrutiny.
Nipple shy but brazen

Taking casual comfort
In the barely mysterious
With potent disdain for the imperfect

Casting stones...
As though impenetrable,
The armor,
remains of pop culture

Even if I were one of them,
I couldn't bear
Having so little left to hide

ACKNOWLEDGEMENTS

I would like to thank my editor, Susan Hughes @ http://myindependenteditor.com. Without her input, I wouldn't have felt quite as confident about releasing these poems on anything but my own website. Also, my husband, Chris for his support and for putting up with all the poetry I've made him read. I would also like to thank all the poets and lyricists who make it okay to write about the not-so-rosy parts of life. Without them, I wouldn't have believed I had anything worth sharing.

About the Author

Shel Craig is a singer, writer and lyricist who resides in Southern Ontario with her drummer husband and two cats.

www.ingramcontent.com/pod-product-compliance
Lightning Source LLC
Chambersburg PA
CBHW071735020426
42331CB00008B/2035